For my favorite little human -
Your courage fills me with pride. You are, and always will be, the reason I found my voice.

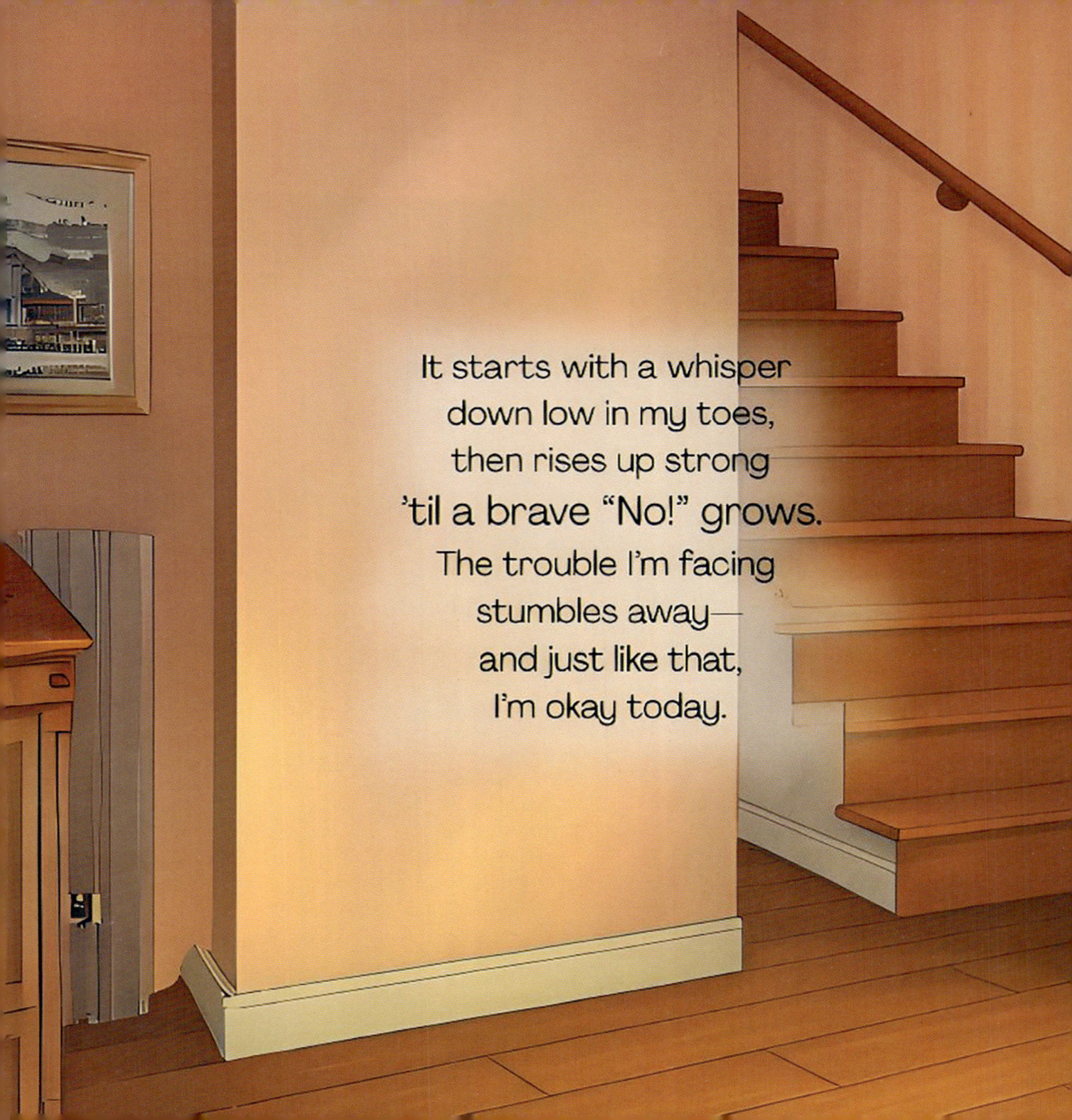
It starts with a whisper
down low in my toes,
then rises up strong
'til a brave "No!" grows.
The trouble I'm facing
stumbles away—
and just like that,
I'm okay today.

RESTROOM

No one can touch me without my say. My
superpower keeps harm away

51A

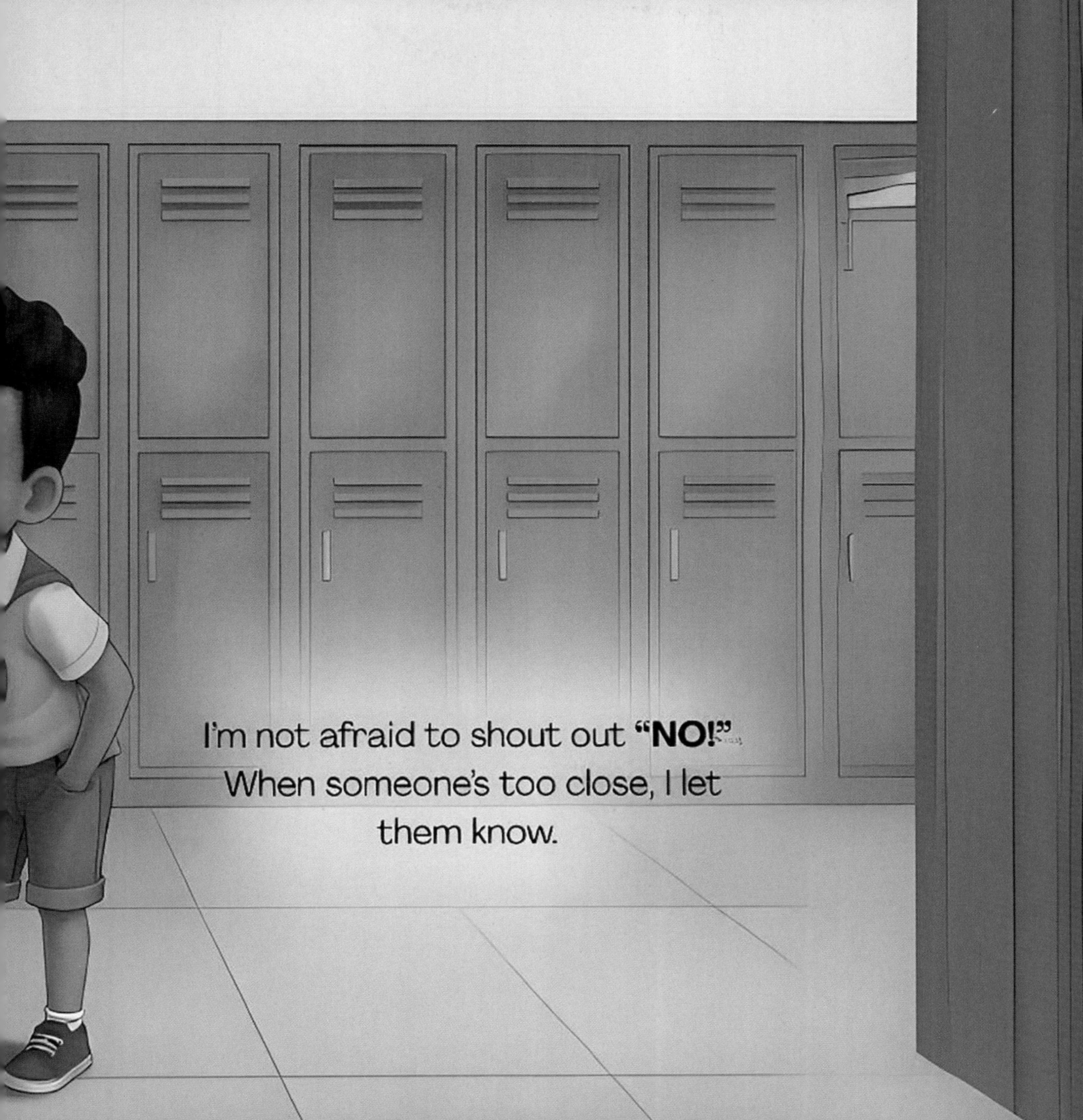

I'm not afraid to shout out **"NO!"**
When someone's too close, I let
them know.

3+2=
What is your n

4. Water
7. Kite
8. Hat
e ?
When something feels off, I know
what to do—I tell an adult who
will help me through.

If I feel afraid or something's not right,
I shout out "NO!" with all of my might.
I take a breath and stand up proud—
My voice is strong, my "NO!" is loud.

When you say "NO," you take control.
It keeps you safe and makes you whole.

Hands should be gentle, kind, and fair.
No one should touch you anywhere.

And if a secret makes you feel bad,
Tell someone trusted—like mom or dad.

If I can be brave, then you can be too.
Here's a quick guide on what you can do.

I use my power when I say "NO!"
It helps me fight and let things go.
Each time I speak, I win the fight—
My voice protects what's good and right.

I'm Body Safety Wise Girl, bold and bright.
And I speak up when things aren't right!

Saying no makes me feel so brave.
I use it whenever I need to be safe.
stops bad things from getting to me,
And builds the hero I'm proud to be.

W

Did you guess what keeps me strong?
It's saying no when something's wrong.
You can use it, yes—it's true,
That mighty word belongs to you!

References

- Briere, J., & Elliott, D, M. (2003). Prevalence and psychological sequelae of self-reported childhood physical and sexual abuse. Child Abuse & Neglect, 27(10),1205-1222.

- Finkelhor, D. (2009). The prevention of childhood sexual abuse. Future of children, 19(2), 169-194.

- Kenny,M.C, & Wurtele,S. K. (2012). Preventing childhood sexual abuse: An evaluation of a teacher training program, Journal of Child Sexual Abuse, 21(4),430-445.

- Sanderson, J. (2004). child-focused sexual abuse prevention programs: How effective are they in protecting children? Trauma, Violence & Abuse, 5(4), 251-268.

- Smallbone.S..Marshal,W.L.,& Wortley,R.(2008).Preventing Child Sexual Abuse: Evidence. Policy and Practice. Willan Publishing.

- Walsh, K, Zwi, K., Woolfenden, s., & shionsky, A. (2015). School-based education programmes for the prevention of child sexual abuse. Cochrane Database of Systematic Reviews, (4)

- Wurtele, s. K., & Kenny, M, c. (2010). Partnering with parents to prevent childhood sexual abuse. Child Abuse Review,19(2),130-152.

- Briere, j.& Elliott,D.(2003).Child Abuse & Neglect, 27(10),1205-1222.

- Finkelhor,D.(2009).Future of Children, 19(2),169-194.

- Kenny, M.& Wurtele, $.(2012). Journal of Child Sexual Abuse, 21(4),430-445.

- Sanderson,].(2004).Trauma, Violence Abuse,5(4),251-268.

- Smallbone, $. et al. (2008). Preventing Child Sexual Abuse: Evidence, Policy and Practice.

- Walsh, K.et al. (2015).Cochrane Database of Systematic Reviews (4).

- Wurtele, S.& Kenny, M.(2010).Child Abuse Review, 19(2),130-152

Resources for Parents

The Reality

1 in 4 girls and 1 in 6 boys will experience sexual abuse before turning 18 (Warrior).

Children between the ages of 12-17 are four times more likely to be victims of rape or sexual assault than adult women(CDC).

In an over whelming 91% of cases, the abuser is someone the child knows and trusts - often a family member,teacher,coach,or close friend(CDC).

Why Early Education Matters

Many types of abuse are subtle and can be hard to recognize. Grooming often starts with kind gesturesgifts --secrets, or extra attention - and esealates slowly, This makes it harder for children to identif what's wrong, and even harder to speak up